MW00667945

If mere mention of a destination's name
Stirs wonder in our soul
Then we must go and learn
Why that is so

Sarasota

A Tribute in Verse and Vision

Jack Veeger and Patricia Nebel

PUBLISHER
Windvane Arts
www.WindavneArts.com

FIRST EDITION: September 2009
ISBN # 978-0-615-29479-7

Printed in the United States of America
Bang Printing
www.BangPrinting.com

COPYRIGHTS
Text Copyright
© 2009 by the Jack Veeger. All Rights Reserved.
Photography Copyright
© 2009 by Patricia Nebel. All Rights Reserved.

All rights reserved. No part of this book may be reproduced or transmitted
in any form or by any means, electronic or mechanical, including photocopying,
recording, or by any information storage and retrieval system, without
written permission from the copyright owners, except for the inclusion of brief
quotations in a review. Permission requests can be sent to info@WindvaneArts.com.

CREDITS
Photograph of Jack Veeeger by Alex of Sarasota, FL.
Photograph of Patricia Nebel by Ron Pluim, Lake Wylie, SC.
The outline of Michelangelo's Statue of David is from the hand of artist Janine Hoffman, Bradenton, FL.
Book layout by Patricia Nebel.

Windvane Arts
Jack Veeger, Patricia Nebel, and Gary Nebel
2477 Stickney Point Road, Suite 121-B
Sarasota, FL 34231

www.WindvaneArts.com
info@WindvaneArts.com

My Love of Town is Not a Paltry Thing

"Vignettes"

My love of town is not a paltry thing
I dote on skyline when the light is timid
I dote on skyline when the light is tired
And when the colors are of fused and singular concoction

...

When people throng to road and ramp
On multitude of arbitrary assignations
Or just the spur of random revelations
We rush, we wait, the sun is full of mercy

...

On Sundays church bells ring in pious competition
And all of faith flock to their kneeling pews
The messages most commonly are stern and somber
But music spilling out onto the streets is pure elation

...

Nowhere on earth are beaches as pristine
The sands as soft, the waters quite as wistful
And always there are breezes that lose time
Inveigle dreams to sneak into day's doings

...

Change mode and manner when the sun hangs high
And heat suggests a slower, wiser pace
A frequent bench in live oak's pensive shade
Too precious is our time to waste it on unruly haste

2

So Tragic and So Touching

Hearts bleed for poor Madama Butterfly
For Mimi and Carmen, for Aida, Lucia and Tosca
For foolish Figaro and Faust, the lusting Scarpia
So much of tragedy and yet we sing and bid goodbye

At curtain fall and fading of the coda in death rattle
We rise and wildly clap and shout as quickly resurrected
Heroes and heroines reappear for grateful bows
And feel relieved that all that dying was but tattle

Back home the arias still echo in our ears
Emotions too flood back and with the tears a want for more
It is the music that regenerates a pleading encore
Each time when we must combat fears

Moods that Tell

I fathom souls by tears as shed
When there is sorrow in the air
When day is dark and I feel poorly led
There seem but pits and grim despair

I fathom souls by smiles as beamed
When songs hang gaily in the air
When sun and moon direct what dreamed
There then is paradise so I declare

Les Oiseaux de Neige
About our ambitious and ambiguous season

Should we not bow and scrape
When the snowbirds land
When they redraw the cityscape
And force the native's hand

Lay on our most audacious menus
And yield to alien license plates
In parking lots and near congested venues
Indeed be gracious hosts to border mates

They pay good money for luxuriating in a sun
That we appear to take for granted
And over which we do not have dominion
It isn't as if we are about to be supplanted

I grant there is occasional inconvenience
What with impatient and assertive crowds
And insufficiency of long-fused patience
But worse than that is a golden sun obscured by clouds

Come on, sweet Sarasota, share and shine
And show the world your trophied worth
Reflect on Caledonian roots and auld lang syne
We are among the envied on this earth

Gone Fishing

Within bay's confines waters babble incoherently
As do the dolphin, blue crab and the snook
And trout and pompano and mullet joining presently
This hour I take from Isaac Walton's book

For still conversing in an alien tongue
With alien creatures hunting for the selfsame key
To alien premonitions – solemnly but not high strung
Assuredly adverse to sounds of war and anarchy

A grouper looks at me with uncommunicative eyes
He sucks in air, looks twice to ascertain, be doubly sure
"Why do so many of you tell so many lies?"
Ashamedly I reel in my offensively misleading lure

Of Glass and Gloss

With aid of sun and sky
The Ritz ran smack into the panels
Of an immobile glass-clad edifice
Across the Trail
And there it stuck
A flattened image
As if enforced upon retentive glass
In sharp and shimmering colors
And smacking of kaleidoscopes and opulence
All luminosity and loveliness
And yet no more than passing gloss

Island Park

There are no burial grounds for gods
But if there were
Most likely they would be
In Sarasota's Island Park

Because it's there
That sky and water meet
In a profusion of pure pleasures

Fair waters that mesmerize
Blue skies that sympathize
The sunset hours that enchant

Mix in the perfumes
Of jasmine and gardenia
Nighttime's seductive spices

And breezes that becalm
Lay cooling hands on brows
And ease discomfort

Like heaven is our Island Park
Port of propriety and peace
Retreat of ultimate resort
And certainly the gods know all about it

The Other Half – The Night Guests of the Park

It is the haggard face of poverty that haunts
When sleep steals furtively across the weariness of bones
And cognizance in single instance slips from harried mind
Last image is of scurrying eyes and pleading unwashed hands

These wayward guests routinely break park's laws
When families and lovers and concert-goers make for home
They stay for they have nowhere else to go or be but here
To themselves they have the grass, the shrubs, the trees and pesky thoughts

Of hunger and worry about the thieves among them
Who prey on fellow fatesakes – among them is no honor –
Uneasy is the sleep that's intermittent in the settling
Another day of conmanship chalked up to wits and wiles

Nearby bay's waters murmur, ripple and cleanse
Red mangrove roots reflect on life with stoic equanimity
The stars beam down with twinkles written all over them
Quite doubtful are night's blessings when sleepers cough and wheeze

Sunday Blues

Life hurts. Please let me sing the blues
So you will know that I bear you no grudge
The blues they ease the pains, the overdues
Perhaps they'll prompt the needed nudge

To right life's arbitrariness in dole
Too much of comfort there too little here
So there is aching in the shorted soul
Please listen to my blues. It's only fair

The church doors stood ajar
So I felt free to enter and to join in pleas
For full egality — a concept from afar
In granting I shall read regret for past inequities

Thank the Oak for Keeping Secrets

I find no fault with bonsai trees
But give me oaks – majestic oaks
As line the streets of Florida's cities
Moss-bearded oaks that stem sun's fiercest strokes

No single-trunk tree as mighty nor as massive
The oak won't hear of being bested
No shade more dense nor more effective
The oak prevails, supreme and storm-tested

It knows its might and tolerates no dare
But as for me I prize the shield that it provides
On afternoons against both heat and glare
And keeping secrets whispered by young brides

Still to Learn

When shall I learn
That every time when I set sail
I leave behind what's dearer than next find

That every time when I return
I wonder what obsessed me to hit trail
Instead of treasuring the bonds that tend and bind

I keep on falling for the lure of next sojourn
That promises a rainbow's end without accustomed fail
So I capitulate and satisfy my soft, manipulative mind

Assuredly time sides with wiser yearn
Some day I'll write a postscript to my tale
In all home's comforts after having wined and dined

Exception to the Rule

In this our land of ramshackle cities and towns
Occasional display of civic pride is doubly hailed
For how it shows without provoking frowns
And too for showing how developers have sadly failed

Where planners kept at bay the urban sharks
There now are monuments and artful niceties
Soft-gurgling fountains, colonnades and parks
Bandstands and statuary and benches under trees

And too bedazzling beaches, dunes and lovers' lanes
Wind-driven waters that beguile and sunsets that benumb
Odd palms and venues for repertories and refrains
This is a languorous place reverberating like a drum

Of Sarasota I now speak
A city on a fabled bay
Where not a single day is bleak
And ease is served on silver tray

Clever Critters

How clever of opossum and raccoon
To take up residence in Oyster Bay
And every night – with coming of the moon
Have access to the garbage from gourmets

Their refuse makes for wholesome waste
Is gobbled up by the nocturnals – young and old
Who pride themselves on their superior taste
And nod when of the finer things in life are told

Of Mayhem and Moderation

No city is complete
Without occasional rains
As they may fall as gentle treat
Or as a torrent causing pains

All parched and sere our town would be
Were rains withheld, diverted or polluted
And green and citrus could not be
Our lives would have to be reconstituted

Upheaval too would be in aftermath of flood
Impassable our roads, uninhabitable our homes
Foul misery because of loss of life and blood
The bees lament the ruin of their honeycombs

To sun we grant more partial leeway
In due dispensing of communal properties
Be they of rain or shine, of night or day
Sun's power has its privileged liberties

Causeway Kitten

A kitten – barely two weeks old –
All black with big and curious eyes
Jumped off our feted banner bridge
And met with solid water sixty plus feet down

It was picked up by town's intrepid rescue team
Accustomed to misfortuned kittens in hot water
It shook itself till dry, then petulantly asked
For consolation milk not liking bay's offensive offering

When much ado was made of mishap and survival
And one reproached the cat for brazen recklessness
It merely shrugged, responded fatuously
"Eight more to go"

Saturday's Farmers Market

Our market is about sweet fragrances
Of herbs and spices, ginger root
Of greenery and fancied fruit
All fresh from tree, prolific plant
Or proffered up by sun-nudged soil
Of wholesomeness of mandarin and berry
Of cauliflower, yam and olive oil

And gay and festive is the market
With multi-mannered music
That hangs and hovers between the walls
As does the breeze that jostles
For a sounding board to trumpet pleasure
With downtown's prim, patrician ambience
Then makes a case for lengthier sojourn

R.I.P.

In time I'll rest in somnolent Memorial Park
Along Route 41 where din of traffic never ceases
But neither sound of ages nor dog's bark
Disturb the peace then free of daft caprices

I'll be content just knowing there are larks
In shading trees that sing full-throated songs
Of praise and merriment, triumphal arcs
That favor rights and waiver wrongs

A visitor may come and drop a daisy past its prime
Just overhead and share with me half of a smile
In the forsaken world such incident shall merit rhyme
And for repeat I probably shall have to wait an eon's while

For now I'll venture out on toxic Tamiami Trail
Contribute to congestion while honking horn
Conveniently argue that chagrin is never to avail
And once I move Route 41 shall cease to be a thorn

Smell the Roses

I judge world's cities by their smell
If I smell pine, cut grass and briny sea
I know that all is good and well
And that the air is fancy-free

One of such cities is beguiling Sarasota
A city of largesse, bonhomie and fandango
Where spite is spurned and vented the vendetta
And work can wait until tomorrow

Should there be lodged a residue of rancor
That irks the sun and also sunshine's hour
Encourage miscreant to haul fouled anchor
Before the rot sets in and air goes sour

On routine day when dusk gains prominence
And sun accedes to ebbing of dominion
All fragrances that hung in condoned reticence
Await dispersing by a wind that wills communion

Let traveler and citizen be
golden in their contemplation

Of all the gifts displayed
on land and water

And gladly shared with
seekers of the peace

This well may be new
Xanadu, enchanted habitation

Unsung must be this city's
unique glories

As they unfold before
beholder's eye

So each observer may
relate in his own words

The praises sung in oft-
repeated stories

St. Armands Circle

We need not tell the honeybees
When clover's bloomings sag
From weight of nectar
The bees they know
In swarms they fall upon the fields
To feast

So too it is with womenfolk
When merchants have restocked
Both shelves and bins
The shoppers know
And come by car or fancy trolley
To feast

Such is perfidious temptation
Of siren called St. Armands Circle

Is This Then Paradise?

Is this then paradise?
Hailed haven for the old, the tired
The truant traveler, the wise
Is this then home as most desired?

Away from lifeless trees
And greens too frigid for concern with bloom
Away from snow and ice, from shiver sprees
And skies preoccupied with morbid gloom

Instead a wooed and winsome sea
Confiding fantasies in whisper tones
Instead a choir of lofty lark and chickadee
Encoding songs with wordless overtones

A place that winds its way into the hearts
Of wayward wanderers, both young and old
A place that captivates as trumps in cards
Allow it to engage in mesmerizing hold

Entitlement

Winds too take winks when done with blowing
And oars are stowed when done with rowing
And we – as winds and oars beseech –
We owe ourselves a respite on Siesta Beach

Our Sun is a Mild and Golden Sun

The sun is mild and golden on our path
Pure luster scattered by a copious hand
No prejudice, no bias and most certainly no wrath
Enfold us, sun, and let us consummate your grant

Our Moon is a Mooning Moon

Each time the moon resembles plump and pampered Yorick
Love blooms to where it even tempts the saint
And we succumb, add piquancy with lusty limerick
And kiss the moon for loosening constraints

Our Stars are Real Stars

The stars of Sarasota's sky are real stars
That blink and twinkle, make you smile
They need not hours to obscure the littlest scars
Moreover powder, paint and puff produce but guile

34

Inscrutable Waters

The sea we call the sing-song Caribbean
Does most of sunning on rickety and muted doorsteps
Sometimes white-knuckled
Sometimes insanely mad
But mostly languid
Contented like a well-fed cat
Yawning, stretching
Dreaming of a coveted fish
Deception by soft purring
Or sparring with a souled steel band
A rumble roll from a calypso drum
And sweating passionate fandangos
Sunset voodoo
Tears and laughter
No one will know

Good at easing
Good at burying of pain

Winds of Woe

Distinctly I heard voices in the wind
That whipped the waters of our bay
Into a foaming fury, frenzied and chagrined
And screamed and shrieked while fanning fray

The waters roiled, rooftops and palms recoiled
And pain and wounds piled up in wake of wreckage
All lifelines snapped and found their functions foiled
Not man nor what man wrought escaped the carnage

The city might as well not be or just play dead
Impassable the roads and lanes and avenues
All littered with debris, spooked wildlife that we dread
This then is foretaste of apocalyptic impromptus

Again I hear wind's voice now impish, tentative
A voice that not of spite, nor hate, nor malice speaks
Just means to say in a conciliatory narrative
"I am haphazard child of nature's wanton freaks"

About Numbering of Days and Hours

So neatly numbered are the grinding hours
With minute numbers within hour numbers
Asserting that in numbers lies a sum of powers
Numbered time for work and numbered time for slumbers

But I'm in Sarasota and wish to not know time of day
So I – once more – can savor some clandestine glee
From truancy and stealing from work to give to play
And not be bothered by a sense of lurid larceny

Should disregard of time prove much too nettlesome
I could agree to slowing down of clock and chime
If that is possible in this our peaceable peopledom
Prime purpose is to find more time inside allotted time

Five Points Junction

At Five Points Junction – one of my city's hearts –
The grass just seems a little greener
Than other grass in other city parts
And too perspective seems a wee bit keener

It's here that I seek time for weighty reading
About some distant problems and nearby worries
About the quality of life we all are leading
And ask "Can we not do without these hurries?"

On days when sun is at its gentlest
I like to read of truths that serve all ages
Of paradise and peace that passes test
And lo a breeze stands by to turn the pages

Of Hail and Harmony

To sing I need not be in glen of songs
To laugh I need not be on hill of laughs
I sing when mood strikes ocean's gongs
I laugh when thoughts are miles from epitaphs

Van Wezel's complex is where arts are all the rage
From tragedy to comedy, marimba and bel canto
They all share curtain calls and kliegs of stage
Famed artist, rising star and vintage virtuoso

All-pleasing is each season's rich and varied repertoire
Indoor or seductively presented under devious stars
And elsewhere orchestra and opera, not far
Engaging are all winds, the harps, the taut guitars

We love the music sprinkled on our city by good muses
It hangs vicariously defying tow and tug from winds
It glorifies. The sunset hours it suffuses
And is but one of Sarasota's finer prints

A Castle for Keepsakes

I slept and conjured up a castle
Not one of crystal nor of marble
And neither ordinary brick and mortar
Instead a castle of fancy filigree
To safekeep and hold free from harm
My lifelong cache of random dreams
Some wet from ill-spilled tears
Some leaving me with blue-black bruises
Some filled with sheer heroics
And many of the wistful type

I built this castle on soft white sand
With winsome waters looking on
And buffeting winds that test the palms
And out of courtesy it may outdally me
By one commiserating day
A private castle without much mass appeal
But crammed with intimate mementos
From bagatelles to mega moments
From rue to almost crass elation
Kaleidoscopic trove of personal minutiae

On covetous Siesta Key this castle stands

Waking Sarasota is Delicate Business

Dawns come to Sarasota on tippy-toes
And without warning to the ones mid-dream
Who do not care to have a pleasure interrupted
For no better reason than coffee and cream

We do not rudely open jalousies and drapes
Lest sunlight enters in profaning stream
Such callousness would never do nor be allowed
More civilized is sun's admission beam by beam

We do not tolerate the ears to be assaulted
At first awareness by traffic's ghastly scream
Obscene would be such paining start to a new day
And no amount of penitence could rightfully redeem

We do not like the mind to be beset by woe
When still in somnolent state – halfway in dream
Halfway in presence – can crude reality not wait
Until we've come to terms with new day's scheme

Sounding Off on Sound

In the ornate expanse of sky
More stars collide and crash
Than ants inhabit tallest hill
Yet of the impact not a decibel is heard

So too the music dies
In infinite space
And over infinite time
And there shall be but eerie silence

Why cannot sound survive
Bounce off nomadic clouds
Send echoes to all corners
And so be heard throughout dust-crusted space

More dear to man is sound
Not light in its gradations
But sound of laughter, sound of tears
We know of sound as we do know of being

Comes that detested day of darkness
When one by one the senses fold
I shall expect to hear that final voice
Proclaiming "Welcome to eternity"

And I shall rest at Sarasota's Memorial Park
Along Route 41 where din of traffic never ceases
And not the sound of ages nor dog's bark
Shall interrupt the peace no longer subject to caprices

By Any Means

How does one travel to presumptive paradise
No road so marked on any map
No town by name of paradise so listed
And yet all talk is of a place called paradise
Like fabled Xanadu and Shangri-la

This paradise is filled to bursting with sun
With flowers, fruit and fancy frill
With waters that gurgle and laugh
And people pinching self for reassurance
This paradise is not just gossamer of dreams

Look under "S"
For Sarasota

41

Had Aesop known our thoroughfare
He would have chosen ignominious 41
As venue for his fabled obstacle course
Which rarely yields a winner
But just surviving is reward enough

Tall Order but Short Shrift

Abnormal is the height
From which some palms look down
Upon the passerby – stunted, midgety and slight –
They – bent and crooked – awkward about town

Each wind takes toll on towering
The selfsame wind that strokes, caresses
That bends the back to point of aching
Insists that we endure life's stresses

I question nature's prowess
Behind this gangly and unsightly stalk
Branchless, leafless, bloomless, clueless
Would not the ugly duckling balk?

Something New and Beautiful Afoot

Do not belabor point of night
Nor vanity of brightest hour
Nor scold the time of day's dark light
When bat and owl venture from their tower

We need reprieve from blood's mad racing
The stress that strains mind's tenure
Review recriminations we keep facing
And sleepily let plantings ripen and mature

Let sun's alluring, filigreed fingers signal dawn
Then rise. Put shoulder to the waiting wheel
Renew old pledges as dew renews the lawn
And golden hours shall befall the ones who kneel

Moon Over Sarasota

A moon – demure and chaste – is plating town with gold
A gently hammered gold that fosters but not touts
Its aim is not to cover up the sores, just to enfold
And to induce soft whisperings to compensate for shouts

On nights like these the bay is sheen and sparkle-rich
Who knows of what the fish may dream and also speak
The charter fleet and sundry yachts show roaming itch
By straining at taut mooring lines that creak

On shore it's time for candles and for wine
A languorous hour not to be disturbed by bagatelle
There's wind in the fronds and perfume masks the brine
So thank the moon and smile as she turns spin and spell

At Will of Wind

Four-winded is our seasonal city
And kindest wind is saved for summer's season
When sun imposes - seemly without pity -
A blister-heat for which there is no reason

And were it not for a commiserating wind
There would be malcontent and grumbling
And city folk might well rescind
All kindly thoughts, instead revert to rumbling

At will of wind are fortitude and haloed mercy
May wind fill sail, cool fevered brow
And carry dreams to minds that play with myth and fancy
Go east, go west as wind and fantasy haphazardly allow

Night Watch

To guard against the chance of harms
Some blooms close up by folding arms
As soon as dark descends
So too does Sarasota

It shields with double panes
It reassures with locks and chains
So sleep will not be interrupted
Not here in Sarasota

Night watchmen walk deserted beats
To question strangers on forbidden streets
Bold trespassing is frowned upon
Taboo in Sarasota

We trust in moon and stellar nights
To cover us with safeguard lights
Yet add confounding gadgets as after all
We treasure Sarasota

Allow the spell cast by these pages to linger
Or better yet
Now you have heard the ring from Sarasota's bells
Rest here and do not fret

Jack Veeger was born in The Netherlands in 1926. At age 27 he emigrated to the U.S.A. and made a career in international trade. He turned to writing poetry after retirement in 1995. He and his wife Bobby (Isabella) make their home in Sarasota, Florida.

Patricia Nebel began her photography career in 2001. Her photography has received numerous awards through juried exhibits and has been published in *National Geographic Adventure* magazine and Florida regional magazines. She and her husband, Gary, live in Sarasota, Florida.